# SOME MAJOR EVENTS IN WORLD WAR II

## THE EUROPEAN THEATER

**1939** SEPTEMBER—Germany invades Poland; Great Britain, France, Australia, & New Zealand declare war on Germany; Battle of the Atlantic begins. NOVEMBER—Russia invades Finland.

**1940** APRIL—Germany invades Denmark & Norway. MAY—Germany invades Belgium, Luxembourg, & The Netherlands; British forces retreat to Dunkirk and escape to England. JUNE—Italy declares war on Britain & France; France surrenders to Germany. JULY—Battle of Britain begins. SEPTEMBER—Italy invades Egypt; Germany, Italy, & Japan form the Axis countries. OCTOBER—Italy invades Greece. NOVEMBER—Battle of Britain over. DECEMBER—Britain attacks Italy in North Africa.

**1941** JANUARY—Allies take Tobruk. FEBRUARY—Rommel arrives at Tripoli. APRIL—Germany invades Greece & Yugoslavia. JUNE—Allies are in Syria; Germany invades Russia. JULY—Russia joins Allies. AUGUST—Germans capture Kiev. OCTOBER—Germany reaches Moscow. DECEMBER—Germans retreat from Moscow; Japan attacks Pearl Harbor; United States enters war against Axis nations.

**1942** MAY—first British bomber attack on Cologne. JUNE—Germans take Tobruk. SEPTEMBER—Battle of Stalingrad begins. OCTOBER—Battle of El Alamein begins. NOVEMBER—Allies recapture Tobruk; Russians counterattack at Stalingrad.

**1943** JANUARY—Allies take Tripoli. FEBRUARY—German troops at Stalingrad surrender. APRIL—revolt of Warsaw Ghetto Jews begins. MAY—German and Italian resistance in North Africa is over; their troops surrender in Tunisia; Warsaw Ghetto revolt is put down by Germany. JULY—allies invade Sicily; Mussolini put in prison. SEPTEMBER—Allies land in Italy; Italians surrender; Germans occupy Rome; Mussolini rescued by Germany. OCTOBER—Allies capture Naples; Italy declares war on Germany. NOVEMBER—Russians recapture Kiev.

**1944** JANUARY—Allies land at Anzio. JUNE—Rome falls to Allies; Allies land in Normandy (D-Day). JULY—assassination attempt on Hitler fails. AUGUST—Allies land in southern France. SEPTEMBER—Brussels freed. OCTOBER—Athens liberated. DECEMBER—Battle of the Bulge.

**1945** JANUARY—Russians free Warsaw. FEBRUARY—Dresden bombed. APRIL—Americans take Belsen and Buchenwald concentration camp; Russians free Vienna; Russians take over Berlin; Mussolini killed; Hitler commits suicide. MAY—Germany surrenders; Goering captured.

## THE PACIFIC THEATER

**1940** SEPTEMBER—Japan joins Axis nations Germany & Italy.

**1941** APRIL—Russia & Japan sign neutrality pact. DECEMBER—Japanese launch attacks against Pearl Harbor, Hong Kong, the Philippines, & Malaya; United States and Allied nations declare war on Japan; China declares war on Japan, Germany, & Italy; Japan takes over Guam, Wake Island, & Hong Kong; Japan attacks Burma.

**1942** JANUARY—Japan takes over Manila; Japan invades Dutch East Indies. FEBRUARY—Japan takes over Singapore; Battle of the Java Sea. APRIL—Japanese overrun Bataan. MAY—Japan takes Mandalay; Allied forces in Philippines surrender to Japan; Japan takes Corregidor; Battle of the Coral Sea. JUNE—Battle of Midway; Japan occupies Aleutian Islands. AUGUST—United States invades Guadalcanal in the Solomon Islands.

**1943** FEBRUARY—Guadalcanal taken by U.S. Marines. MARCH—Japanese begin to retreat in China. APRIL—Yamamoto shot down by U.S. Air Force. MAY—U.S. troops take Aleutian Islands back from Japan. JUNE—Allied troops land in New Guinea. NOVEMBER—U.S. Marines invade Bougainville & Tarawa.

**1944** FEBRUARY—Truk liberated. JUNE—Saipan attacked by United States. JULY—battle for Guam begins. OCTOBER—U.S. troops invade Philippines; Battle of Leyte Gulf won by Allies.

**1945** JANUARY—Luzon taken; Burma Road won back. MARCH—Iwo Jima freed. APRIL—Okinawa attacked by U.S. troops; President Franklin Roosevelt dies; Harry S. Truman becomes president. JUNE—United States takes Okinawa. AUGUST—atomic bomb dropped on Hiroshima; Russia declares war on Japan; atomic bomb dropped on Nagasaki. SEPTEMBER—Japan surrenders.

# WORLD AT WAR

# Invasion
# of Russia

# WORLD AT WAR

# Invasion
# of Russia

By R. Conrad Stein

Consultant:
Professor Robert L. Messer, Ph.D.
Department of History
University of Illinois, Chicago

**ℂℙ** CHILDRENS PRESS ™

CHICAGO

German troops cross the Bug River as the invasion of Russia begins.

**Library of Congress Cataloging in Publication Data**

Stein, R. Conrad.
  Invasion of Russia.

  (World at war)
  Summary: Traces the events of the German invasion of Russia in the summer and winter of 1941–1942.
  1. World War, 1939–1945—Campaigns—Soviet Union—Juvenile literature. 2. Soviet Union—History—German occupation, 1941–1944—Juvenile literature. [1. World War, 1939–1945—Campaigns—Soviet Union. 2. Soviet Union—History—German occupation, 1941–1944]
I. Title.  II. Series.
D764.S865  1985    940.54′21    84-23231
ISBN 0-516-04778-7

FRONTISPIECE:
A German grenade thrower contributes to the destruction of a Russian village.

PICTURE CREDITS:
WIDE WORLD PHOTOS: Cover, 19 (top), 22
NATIONAL ARCHIVES: Pages 4, 6, 9, 16, 23, 28, 41 (top), 44, 45
SOVFOTO: Pages 10, 29, 30, 35, 38, 39, 46
UPI: Pages 12, 13, 15, 19 (bottom), 24, 25, 27, 32, 37, 40, 41 (bottom), 42, 43
LEN MEENTS (MAP): Page 20

COVER PHOTO: German machine gunners somewhere on the Russian front defending a bridge from attack from the houses in the background

PROJECT EDITOR:
Joan Downing

CREATIVE DIRECTOR:
Margrit Fiddle

Rumors swept like fire through the ranks of German troops stationed along the Bug River in occupied Poland. "We're going on a big maneuver." "We're going to be transferred west to invade England." Only a few soldiers dared to suggest, "We're going to attack Russians."

The rumors were fueled by recent troop movements that assembled entire German divisions along the Russian frontier. Huge stores of ammunition and gasoline were stockpiled. This massive operation was carried out in the strictest secrecy. Trucks and tanks moved only at night, and their drivers were ordered to keep the headlights off. By mid-June, 1941, three million soldiers had gathered in the Polish forests along a 930-mile border separating the German and Russian forces. Some of the men on the German side came from Hungary and Rumania, allies of Germany. But the overwhelming majority of the troops were German.

On the evening of June 21, company commanders assembled their men to read an order written by Adolf Hitler himself. It began, "Soldiers of the Eastern Front!" The Eastern Front? Where is this Eastern Front? the men wondered. The proclamation continued, "For weeks our frontier has been violated continually." The men were told of numerous Russian patrols into German territory that were driven back only after violent firefights. "German soldiers! You are about to join a battle, a hard and crucial battle. The destiny of Europe and the future of Germany now lie in your hands alone."

Hitler's order ended the rumors. Tomorrow the men would fight Russians.

June 21, 1941 was a night of clock-watching. No one slept. Pitch darkness still reigned when the clocks ticked to 0315 (3:15 A.M.). Then, along a front that stretched the length of Europe, artillery commanders shouted out a one-word order:

"FIRE!"

German Stuka dive-bombers raced to targets deep inside Soviet territory.

Some six thousand huge German guns thundered, belched fire, and spat out their deadly shells. The earth seemed to dance. Below the screaming shells, tank treads clanged as a massive armored force—almost 2,500 tanks—rolled forward. In the air, German fighter planes and dive-bombers swept over the border and raced to targets deep inside Soviet territory.

This Russian village was completely destroyed by
the Germans during the first day of the invasion.

By crossing the frontier, Adolf Hitler launched
the greatest military assault in world history. In
the number of men and machines involved, it
dwarfed even the massive D-Day invasion of
France that would take place three years later.
The Russian adventure was also Hitler's greatest
gamble. Hitler was a student of history. He
knew that the great French leader Napoleon had
once tried, and failed, to conquer the vast lands
of Russia, and that thought haunted him.

However, the conquest of Russia was vital to Hitler's plan to establish a German state that would last a thousand years. In speech after speech, Hitler insisted that overcrowded Germany needed *Lebensraum* (living room). Sprawling Russia, which covered one sixth of the world's surface, had all the *Lebensraum* Hitler coveted.

The attack caught the Russians completely by surprise. One Russian commander radioed his headquarters, "I'm being fired upon. What shall I do?" His superior officer, who was stationed miles from the fighting, radioed back, "You must be insane! No one is firing at you."

Thousands of Russian prisoners were captured by the Germans during the first few months of the German offensive.

Even the Germans were astounded at how unprepared their foes were for battle. German infantrymen attacked bunkers that were empty and trenches that were only half-dug. Those Russian units that did fight put up some splendid battles. But along most of the Eastern Front, the enemy seemed to be in a state of shock. Many of the defenders gave up without firing a shot. When curious Germans asked their prisoners why they did not fight, the bewildered Russians replied, "We had orders never to fire toward the German side."

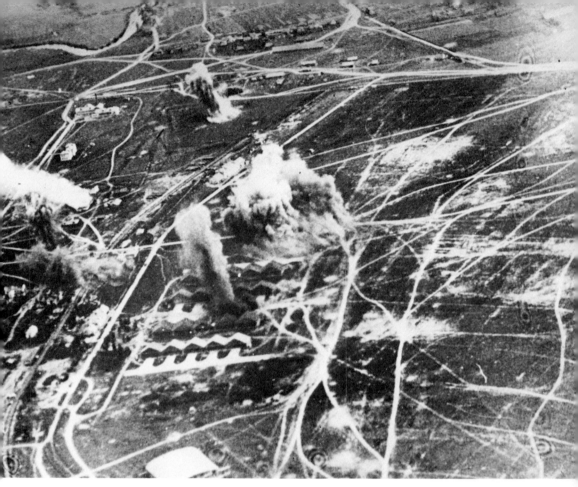

Russian airfields were among the main targets
of German fighters and bombers.

In the air, the surprise attack had even more
dramatic results. German fighters and bombers
struck primarily at the enemy airfields strung out
along the border. Before noon of the first day,
the Germans destroyed twelve hundred Russian
planes. Eight hundred of them were knocked out
on the ground. German losses totaled only ten
aircraft.

Why was the Russian military so woefully unprepared for the German attack? Certainly the German buildup was conducted in secrecy. But it is impossible to assemble three million men and thousands of noisy tanks and trucks without tipping off a foe. To understand how the Russians succumbed to such a stunning surprise, it is necessary to examine history and to probe into the mind of the Russian ruler—Joseph Stalin.

Stalin was born in bitter poverty, but rose to become absolute dictator of Russia. He ruled his country with terror and force. Stalin was a lonely man who believed he had enemies lurking everywhere. He dealt with his enemies—both real and imagined—swiftly and brutally. Under his reign, political rivals were jailed and executed.

Joseph Stalin, absolute dictator of Russia during World War II, ruled his country with terror and force.

For more than a decade, Stalin and Hitler had engaged in a peculiar cat-and-mouse game. Certainly their political philosophies were dramatically opposed to one another. But in the 1930s, both Russia and Germany were the outcasts of Europe. One was Europe's only Communist country; the other was the major loser of World War I. So Germany and Russia grudgingly cooperated in trade and other agreements. Finally, on August 23, 1939, Stalin signed a nonaggression pact with Hitler. Stalin promised to remain neutral if the Germans went to war. The two dictators also secretly agreed to divide Poland between them.

German Foreign Minister Joachim von Ribbentrop (left), Russian Foreign Minister V. M. Molotov (right), and Stalin (center) at the signing of the German-Russian nonaggression pact on August 23, 1939.

The nonaggression pact was a diplomatic triumph for Adolf Hitler. If he had to fight France or Great Britain, the pact assured that he could do so without worrying about the Russians. On September 1, 1939, only nine days after signing the agreement, German troops smashed into Poland and World War II began in Europe. On September 17, Russia invaded Poland from the east. Before the month was over, Germany and Russia had divided the defeated country between them.

While Germany achieved further victories on the battlefield, Stalin did nothing to offend Hitler. He mistrusted Hitler, but he mistrusted the French and British leaders even more. For reasons that are still debated by historians, Stalin chose to cooperate with Hitler during the German leader's early struggles with the West. The Soviet Union became Germany's primary supplier of grain and war materials. In fact, a Soviet train hauling tons of grain to Germany crossed the frontier at 2:00 A.M. on June 22— little more than an hour before the attack.

Hoping to maintain the precarious peace with Hitler, Stalin ordered his commanders along the frontier not to provoke the Germans in any way. The border "violations" that Hitler used as an excuse to attack Russia were pure fabrications.

Actually, Stalin's desire to avoid upsetting the Germans was the major reason why the Russian army was so helpless to repel the surprise invasion once it was underway. It was not until 7:15 A.M.—after four hours of fighting—that Stalin officially allowed his commanders to fire back if they were fired upon. Even then, he refused to permit his men to counterattack and enter German-held territory. By that time, however, the notion of counterattacking was a wild dream. The Soviet army reeled backward in the face of a relentless German onslaught.

*Blitzkrieg*. In German the word means "lightning war." *Blitzkrieg* is an offensive plan of action in which tanks and motorized infantry, covered by massed air forces, break through an enemy's front lines and thunder into its rear positions. The concept of *Blitzkrieg* was first tested in Poland, then perfected in France. By the time of the invasion of Russia, the Germans were masters at waging lightning war.

The German tanks pictured above rolled on without much difficulty during the early months of the *Blitzkrieg*, but army trucks (below) had a hard time moving over Russia's bumpy, all but nonexistent, roads.

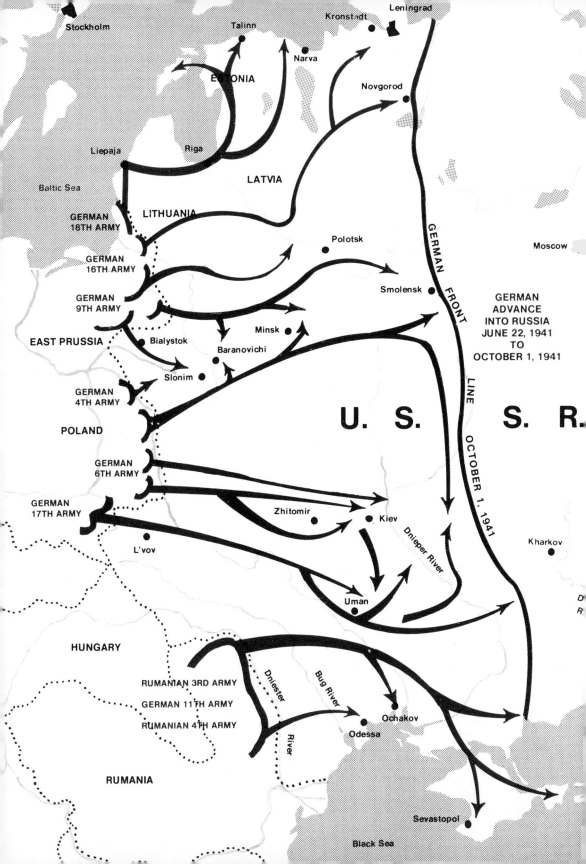

Stockholm

Talinn

Kronstadt

Leningrad

Narva

ESTONIA

Novgorod

Liepaja

Riga

LATVIA

Baltic Sea

GERMAN
18TH ARMY

LITHUANIA

Polotsk

Moscow

GERMAN
16TH ARMY

Smolensk

GERMAN
FRONT

GERMAN
9TH ARMY

Minsk

GERMAN
ADVANCE
INTO RUSSIA
JUNE 22, 1941
TO
OCTOBER 1, 1941

EAST PRUSSIA

Bialystok

Baranovichi

LINE

Slonim

U. S.

S. R.

GERMAN
4TH ARMY

OCTOBER 1, 1941

POLAND

GERMAN
6TH ARMY

GERMAN
17TH ARMY

Zhitomir

Kiev

L'vov

Kharkov

Dnieper River

Uman

D
R

HUNGARY

RUMANIAN 3RD ARMY

Dniester

Bug River

GERMAN 11TH ARMY

RUMANIAN 4TH ARMY

River

Ochakov

Odessa

RUMANIA

Sevastopol

Black Sea

The offensive's code name was "Operation Barbarossa," in honor of a medieval German prince who successfully defeated his enemies in the East. During the initial battles, it appeared that the Germans would again triumph over their Eastern foes. By the fifth day of the operation, German armored columns had smashed 150 miles into Soviet territory.

Clever German generals used ingenious methods to keep their weapons of *Blitzkrieg* rolling. At one point on the Bug River, a unit of German tanks crossed where there was no bridge. Engineers accomplished this miracle by outfitting eighty tanks with special watertight seals and long snorkel hoses. This enabled the tanks to cross *under* the water by crawling over the riverbed. Near the city of Daugava, a company of German soldiers disguised themselves in Russian uniforms, drove captured Russian trucks right through enemy lines, and took a key bridge.

Russian infantry troops, supported by tanks, attack German fortifications.

But the Germans quickly discovered that they had underestimated the strength of the Russian army. Before the invasion, they had calculated that the Russians had 213 divisions in the field. Once they began fighting their way through Russian territory, the Germans encountered units they didn't know existed. Actually, Stalin's forces totaled 360 divisions. Furthermore, the Germans found to their horror that the Soviet army had tanks that were far more powerful than their own.

The first new Russian tanks the Germans encountered were the KV-1 and KV-2 series. Weighing forty-three and fifty-two tons respectively, they were about twice the size of Germany's heaviest tanks. Their thick armored plating made these monsters almost invincible in

The destruction of this fifty-two-ton Russian KV tank was a cause for celebration—it was the first the Germans were able to destroy.

the field. A member of the German First Panzer Division described his unit's first fight with the powerful Soviet tanks: "The KV-1 and 2, which we first met here, were really something! Our companies opened fire at about 800 yards, but it was ineffective. We moved closer and closer to the enemy, who continued to approach us unconcerned. Very soon we were facing each other at 50 to 100 yards. A fantastic exchange of fire took place. . . . The Russian tanks continued to advance and all [our] shells simply bounced off them."

Cossack horsemen with flashing sabers follow a Red Army tank into battle as Soviet planes roar low overhead. Though this was a fairly efficient combination of Russia's modern and ancient weapons of attack, the Russians later learned from the Germans to use their infantry to support waves of tanks.

Only a tactical error prevented the giant Russian tanks from routing the Germans. The Russians deployed their tanks three, four, and five at a time. They believed the role of tanks was to support infantry. The *Blitzkrieg*-minded German generals believed the reverse; that infantry should support tanks. Later in the war, Russian generals swung over to the German way of thinking. They used waves of their splendid tanks to create an unstoppable Soviet juggernaut.

This young Soviet machine gunner is ready for action.

The Germans also learned to respect the stubborn courage of the Russian fighting man. The Russian fortress at Brest-Litovsk held out for weeks, even though it was surrounded. Using a nail on a concrete wall, one Soviet defender scratched out the words: "We are three men from Moscow—Ivanov, Stepanchikov, and Shuntyayev. We are defending this [bunker] and we have sworn not to surrender. July, 1941." Another note written on the same wall several days later, said: "I am alone now. Stepanchikov and Shuntyayev have been killed. The Germans are inside. I have one hand grenade left. They shall not get me alive."

Despite brave troops and superb tanks, the Russian army was plagued by poor leadership. This leadership crisis can be blamed on the gloomy personality of Joseph Stalin.

Before the war, Stalin had begun to suspect that his army officers planned to overthrow him. Starting in 1937, he launched a great purge of his officer corps. Officers were arrested, accused of plotting against the regime, and then shot after brief trials. In all, 35,000 professional soldiers were executed. Many of them were the nation's brightest generals and military planners. They were replaced by less-competent men whose only qualification for leadership was blind obedience to Stalin. This great purge of military officers severely damaged the spirit of the Russian army.

This Russian town was totally destroyed as the German *Blitz* passed through.

The second week of fighting in Russia saw German armored columns streaking deep into Soviet territory. The German forces were divided into three army groups—north, central, and south. The goal of the northern army was to race along the Baltic Sea and capture Leningrad. Moscow was the target of the central army. The southern army was to occupy the oil-rich Caucasus Mountains. These objectives were the subject of much debate between Hitler and his generals. As Operation Barbarossa intensified, Hitler changed emphasis from one goal to another, time after time, with disastrous results for Germany.

General Heinz Guderian (second from right) was
a commander of the German central army group.

One of the commanders in the central army
group was the brilliant general Heinz Guderian.
More than any other man in the German army
he was responsible for the development of the
tank corps. A firm believer in *Blitzkrieg,* he liked
to say, "Only movement brings us victory." His
men often called him "Hurrying Heinz." Day
after day, Guderian could be found in his
armored command vehicle racing at the head of
his tanks. The words that seemed always on his
lips were, "Keep going! Keep going!"

Soviet troops attacking German tanks

    As their tanks rolled over Russian wheat fields, Guderian and other German generals attempted to execute "pincer movements." To picture a pincer movement, imagine the claws of a giant crab. Think of the claws as swift armored columns that break through an enemy's front lines, meet at a point far to the rear, and trap masses of troops.

The ancient city of Velizh, in the Smolensk region, once renowned for its flourishing gardens, was devastated by the German *Blitzkrieg*.

On July 16, 1941, two German armored columns met at the ancient city of Smolensk in central Russia. The pocket created by the converging claws trapped 100,000 Russian soldiers, 2,000 tanks, and 1,900 guns. At Smolensk, the tanks rumbled over a road that led to the prime objective of the German generals. Alongside this road, a German soldier nailed a hand-painted sign to a tree. It pointed east and said, "Moscow, 200 miles."

While the Germans stormed into the heart of Russia, the world press claimed that the Soviet cause was lost. In a July 28 article entitled THE GERMAN ARMY HEADS FOR MOSCOW, *Life* magazine said, "This war proves once again what nearly everybody has long known: that the German army of 1941 is the greatest fighting outfit ever assembled. Germany was last week decisively beating Soviet Russia. The only remaining doubts were how much of an army the Russians would still have east of Moscow and how long they would trouble to fight there." Newspapers in Great Britain also predicted a quick Russian collapse.

But with victory seemingly in his grasp, Hitler changed his mind.

Adolf Hitler, on a visit to the Russian front, shakes hands
with his southern commander, Field Marshal Gerd von Rundstedt.

In Berlin, the German leader decided against
Moscow being the army's primary objective.
Instead, he resolved that the northern city of
Leningrad must fall first. He tranferred men and
tanks away from the central front and sent them
north. When Leningrad's defenses held firm,
Hitler determined that the vast lands of the
Ukraine, to the south, must be occupied. Again
he shifted forces out of the central front, and this
time sent them south.

The generals in the field fumed. To a man, they wanted to strike directly at Moscow with all the forces they could muster. Moscow was the heart and brain of the Soviet Union. Not only was the city the Soviet capital, it was also a major railroad and manufacturing center. And Moscow's capitulation would be a devasting blow to the morale of the average Russian soldier.

In late August, the generals persuaded Heinz Guderian to go to Berlin and plead their case for an all-out attack on Moscow. The meeting between Guderian and Hitler was perhaps the most fateful conference of World War II. Hitler listened to Guderian's arguments. Then, according to Guderian, "Hitler began to speak. He designated the industrial area about Leningrad as his primary objective. . . . He also believed that the raw materials and agricultural produce of the Ukraine were necessary to Germany for the future prosecution of the war." The Nazi leader was unshakable. The attack on Moscow would have to wait.

In the decades that have passed since 1941, scholars have debated endlessly about what might have happened had Hitler concentrated on a Moscow offensive as his generals had urged him to do. Would Germany have captured Moscow and knocked Russia out of the war? How would the map of Europe have changed? These are the kinds of questions that make history such an interesting subject to study.

After his conference, Guderian returned to the front and led his troops on a new offensive into the Ukraine. Once again, the Germans enjoyed a smashing string of victories. During a great pincer movement at the city of Kiev, the Russians lost a shocking one million men killed, wounded, or taken prisoner.

The German pincer movement that destroyed the city of Kiev (above) also cost the Russians one million men killed, wounded, or taken prisoner.

Success in the Ukraine left Hitler giddy with confidence. He sent his generals a new memo announcing that "the last great decisive battle of the year will mean the annihilation of the enemy." Finally, he ordered a full-scale advance on Moscow. The generals, however, wondered if the decision had come too late.

From the beginning, timing had been a crucial factor in Operation Barbarossa. Hitler and his generals had planned to start the invasion on May 15 instead of in late June. But the invasion date was put back more than a month because Hitler had to send German forces to Yugoslavia in order to rescue his Italian ally Benito Mussolini, who had launched an invasion there. Now the month-long delay worried the generals. Would they have to wage their last offensive in the teeth of the brutal Russian winter?

Soviet guerrilla forces played an important part during the war with the Germans. This group of guerrillas is listening to last-minute instructions before a night raid on German rear forces.

In early October, the German generals assembled their forces for what they hoped would be the last offensive of the war, Before the invasion, the German high command had estimated that it would take only eight weeks to beat the Russians. Already Operation Barbarossa was three months old, and the Germans had lost almost 500,000 men. The surviving troops were exhausted and their equipment was wearing out.

The Soviet *Katyusha* multiple-rocket launcher was called Stalin's Pipe Organ.

Adding to the German woes, the Russians
began to unleash their most terrifying new
weapons. One of these was the *Katyusha*
multiple-rocket launcher that could fire a dozen
or more high-explosive shells all at once.
Because of its pipes and the high-pitched sound
made by the rockets, German soldiers called
this weapon Stalin's Pipe Organ. Russian
General A. I. Yeremenko wrote: "We first tried
out this superb weapon at Rudnya north-west
of Smolensk. . . . Like red-tailed comets the
rockets were hurled into the air. The effect of
the simultaneous explosions of dozens of these
shells was terrific. The Germans fled in panic."

The Soviet T-34 tank was called the best tank in World War II.

The Russians also brought to the front their newest tank, the T-34. Many tank experts, including Guderian, called the T-34 the best tank in World War II. It had thick sloping armor and a lethal 76mm gun that could knock out a German tank with one shot. Although it weighed a bulky thirty tons, the T-34's very wide caterpillar treads enabled it to plow across muddy fields in which even lighter tanks became mired.

During the advance on Moscow, the nature of the fighting grew to a savage ferocity. These German machine gunners were grim, ruthless killers.

During the advance on Moscow, the nature of the fighting grew uglier. From the beginning, Hitler had ordered his generals to ignore any crimes that a German soldier might commit against Russian civilians or prisoners of war. Consequently, prisoners were shot, villages were burned, and women were attacked. The Russians, too, shot and tortured German prisoners. All wars are cruel, but the Russian-German conflict sank to the level of primitive barbarism.

One bloody day followed another as the German war machine pushed toward the Soviet capital. Russian resistance stiffened. The Germans attacked with savage ferocity. Casualties on both sides mounted at an appalling rate.

In an attempt to leave nothing behind that the advancing German army could use, Stalin followed a "scorched-earth" policy. Russians were ordered to burn their homes and fields before the Germans reached their villages (above). In retaliation, thousands of Russian peasants were shot by invading Germans (left).

"General Mud" took over when the late October rains halted the German advance.

In late October, fall rains drenched the battlefield. Roads turned into rivers of gluelike mud that stopped the German armored columns. While the German tanks slipped and skidded in the mire, the wide-track Russian T-34s still rolled and blazed away at the stalled enemy vehicles. German commanders prayed that cold weather would freeze the ground so they could continue their offensive. When the cold did come, it hit like a blow from a hammer.

A bone-chilling cold snap struck the Moscow area in November. Temperatures plunged almost to zero. Icy winds whistled over the fields. Still the Germans pressed on. The last hundred miles that took them to the outskirts of Moscow cost the German army a quarter of a million men.

A horse-drawn German soup kitchen fords a flooded area on its perilous way to the front.

The German troops advancing on Moscow in November bore little resemblance to the confident, well-equipped soldiers who had invaded Russia in June. With their supply lines stretched out over two thousand miles, German infantrymen were short on food and ammunition. Because the high command had expected the war to be over by the end of summer, most German soldiers had no winter coats or boots. Frostbite caused more casualties than enemy bullets. During the dismal winter campaign, Guderian wrote to his wife, "I frequently cannot sleep at night and my brain goes round and round while I try to think of what more I can do to help my poor soldiers who are out there without shelter in this abominable cold. It is frightful, unimaginable. The people [in Berlin], who have never seen the front, have no idea what conditions here are like."

This cemetery in Manelja holds only a few of the thousands
of German soldiers who perished in Russia during World War II.

On a snowy morning in December, 1941, a
German patrol climbed a hill ten miles from
central Moscow. Through binoculars, the
soldiers saw the spires of the Kremlin. That was
as close as the German army ever got to the
Russian capital. That afternoon, a massive
Russian counterattack drove them back. For the
very first time in World War II, the German
army failed to achieve a major objective.

Savage battles raged between German and
Russian forces for the next four years. The
Eastern Front, once unknown to German troops,
became every soldier's most dreaded nightmare.
Fully 80 percent of all the casualties the German
army suffered in World War II occurred in the
East.

This Russian poster was an announcement that Adolf Hitler would suffer the same devastating defeat that Emperor Napoleon of France had suffered a century before while trying to conquer the vast lands of Russia. "So was Napoleon and so Hitler will be," the poster proclaims.

Adolf Hitler was a corporal during the First World War. When he invaded Russia, he followed the footsteps of Napoleon, another ambitious ex-corporal. A century earlier, Napoleon's army had seemed unbeatable, and the French leader was on the brink of conquering all of Europe. Then Napoleon suffered a devastating defeat in the snowy fields near Moscow. Napoleon never recovered from the blow he received at Moscow's gates, and neither did Hitler. In 1945, Russian tanks thundered into Berlin, ending Hitler's dream of *Lebensraum* and of a Nazi German state that would last a thousand years.

In a fitting end to Hitler's dream of *Lebensraum* and a Nazi German state that would last a thousand years, Russian tanks thundered into Berlin in April, 1945, and triumphant Russian soldiers raised the Soviet flag over the Reichstag.

# Index

*About the Author*

   Mr. Stein was born and grew up in Chicago. At eighteen he enlisted in the Marine Corps where he served three years. He was a sergeant at discharge. He later received a B.A. in history from the University of Illinois and an M.F.A. from the University of Guanajuato in Mexico.
   Although he served in the Marines, Mr. Stein believes that wars are a dreadful waste of human life. He agrees with a statement once uttered by Benjamin Franklin: "There never was a good war or a bad peace." But wars are all too much a part of human history. Mr. Stein hopes that some day there will be no more wars to write about.